AIR FRYER

Cookbook

The Complete Air Fryer Cookbook
Healthy and Delicious Recipes for
Burning Fat, Boosting Metabolism
and Achieving Rapid Weight Loss

TABLE OF CONTENTS

INTRODUCTION

Air Fryers have many perks to offer when it comes to improving quality of life. It helps in maintaining your wellness and fitness.

Versatile Options

Air Fryer allows you cook a diverse range of foods, be it chicken tenders, mushrooms, crispy fries, fried shrimp, mozzarella sticks, or grilled vegetables. You want to grill, fry, roast, or bake your foods? Air Fryers are there to prepare them in real quick time. Specific ultra-modern range of Air Fryers also allow you make many recipes in a single cooking session.

Superfast Heating

Unlike traditional frying method, Air Fryers takes only a few minutes to heat and prepare foods. They are always ready to make meals whenever you crave for fried foods. Most Air Fryer models get ready in only 3 minutes to heat up properly and they can also go as high as 400 degrees F to make you crispy meals.

Natural Food Taste

It's quite common for anyone to worry about their food's ability to delight them with their mouthwatering flavors. When it comes to Air Fryers, things are no different. Air Fryers prepare meals without compromising on their taste profile. As far as the taste is concerned, they can easily be compared with deep-fried foods.

Time Saving

With only 24 hours to complete everyday routine tasks, the time has become a genuinely luxury in our fast-paced lifestyle. Air Fryers are designed to save your precious cooking time by serving you crunchy snacks and fried cuisines in a matter of minutes. If you are always on a tight schedule, Air Fryer is no less than a time savior.

Space Saver and Ease of Cleaning

Cleaning after cooking foods is also very easy as they are designed for effortless cleaning. On top of that, they don't take up much of your counter space and require quite less space to store.

Useful Tips to Prepare Healthy Foods

- Vegetables are one of the easiest foods to cook in Air Fryer. A wide variety of plants can be cooked, be it delicate beans to root vegetables. For the best cooking experience, firstly, soak the vegetables, especially the harder ones, in cold water for 15-20 minutes. Then after, dry them using a clean kitchen towel.

- Keep in mind that you should always aim to cook your food to desired doneness because the recipes are flexible, and they are designed for all Air Fryer models. If you feel that the food needs more cooking time, then adjust it and cook for a few more minutes. It is not a thumb rule to stick to recipe time only as certain ingredients can vary in their size and firmness from one country to another.

- Roasting with air is a new cooking trend you have to try because you can finally prepare your winter favorites.

- You can bake your favorite recipes in your Air Fryer but always check with the machine's manual before using new baking ware with Air Fryer.

- When it comes to the cooking time, it changes depending on particular Air Fryer model, the size of food, food pre-preparation and so on. For shorter cooking cycles, you should preheat Air Fryer for about 3-4 minutes; otherwise, if you put the ingredients into the cold cooking basket, the cooking time needs to be increased to 3 additional minutes.

- Use a good quality oil spray to brush food and cooking basket; it is also helpful for easy cleanup.

BREAKFAST

Bacon, Egg, and Cheese Roll Ups

Preparation Time: 15 minutes

Cooking Time: 15 minutes

Servings: 4

Ingredients:

- 2 tablespoons unsalted butter
- ¼ cup chopped onion
- ½ medium green bell pepper, seeded and chopped
- 6 large eggs
- 12 slices sugar-free bacon
- 1 cup shredded sharp Cheddar cheese
- ½ cup mild salsa, for dipping

Directions:

1. In a medium skillet over medium heat, melt butter. Add onion and pepper to the skillet and sauté until fragrant and onions are translucent, about 3 minutes.
2. Whisk eggs in a small bowl and pour into skillet. Scramble eggs with onions and peppers until fluffy and fully cooked, about 5 minutes. Remove from heat and set aside.
3. On work surface, place three slices of bacon side by side, overlapping about ¼". Place ¼ cup scrambled eggs in a heap on the side closest to you and sprinkle ¼ cup cheese on top of the eggs.

4. Tightly roll the bacon around the eggs and secure the seam with a toothpick if necessary. Place each roll into the air fryer basket.
5. Adjust the temperature to 350°F and set the timer for 15 minutes. Rotate the rolls halfway through the cooking time.
6. Bacon will be brown and crispy when completely cooked. Serve immediately with salsa for dipping.

Nutrition: Calories: 460 Protein: 28.2 g Fiber: 0.8 g Net carbohydrates: 5.3 g Fat: 31.7 g Sodium: 1,100 mg Carbohydrates: 6.1 g Sugar: 3.1 g

Cheesy Cauliflower Hash Browns

Preparation Time: 20 minutes

Cooking Time: 12 minutes

Servings: 4

Ingredients:

- 1 (12-ounce) steamer bag cauliflower
- 1 large egg
- 1 cup shredded sharp Cheddar cheese

Directions:

1. Place bag in microwave and cook according to package instructions. Allow to cool completely and put cauliflower into a cheesecloth or kitchen towel and squeeze to remove excess moisture.
2. Mash cauliflower with a fork and add egg and cheese.
3. Cut a piece of parchment to fit your air fryer basket. Take ¼ of the mixture and form it into a hash brown patty shape. Place it onto the parchment and into the air fryer basket, working in batches if necessary.
4. Adjust the temperature to 400°F and set the timer for 12 minutes.
5. Flip the hash browns halfway through the cooking time. When completely cooked, they will be golden brown. Serve immediately.

Nutrition: Calories: 153 Protein: 10.0 g Fiber: 1.7 g Net carbohydrates: 3.0 g Fat: 9.5 g Sodium: 225 mg Carbohydrates: 4.7 g Sugar: 1.8 g

Breakfast Stuffed Poblanos

Preparation Time: 15 minutes

Cooking Time: 15 minutes

Servings: 4

Ingredients:

- ½ pound spicy ground pork breakfast sausage
- 4 large eggs
- 4 ounces full-fat cream cheese, softened
- ¼ cup canned diced tomatoes and green chiles, drained
- 4 large poblano peppers
- 8 tablespoons shredded pepper jack cheese
- ½ cup full-fat sour cream

Directions:

1. In a medium skillet over medium heat, crumble and brown the ground sausage until no pink remains. Remove sausage and drain the fat from the pan. Crack eggs into the pan, scramble, and cook until no longer runny.

2. Place cooked sausage in a large bowl and fold in cream cheese. Mix in diced tomatoes and chiles. Gently fold in eggs.

3. Cut a 4"–5" slit in the top of each poblano, removing the seeds and white membrane with a small knife. Separate the filling into four servings and spoon carefully into each pepper. Top each with 2 tablespoons pepper jack cheese.

4. Place each pepper into the air fryer basket.

5. Adjust the temperature to 350°F and set the timer for 15 minutes.

6. Peppers will be soft and cheese will be browned when ready. Serve immediately with sour cream on top.

Nutrition: Calories: 489 Protein: 22.8 g Fiber: 3.8 g Net carbohydrates: 8.8 g Fat: 35.6 g Sodium: 746 mg Carbohydrates: 12.6 g Sugar: 2.9 g

Air Fryer "Hard-Boiled" Eggs

Preparation Time: 2 minutes

Cooking Time: 18 minutes

Servings: 4

Ingredients:

- 4 large eggs
- 1 cup water

Directions:

1. Place eggs into a 4-cup round baking-safe dish and pour water over eggs. Place dish into the air fryer basket.
2. Adjust the temperature to 300°F and set the timer for 18 minutes.
3. Store cooked eggs in the refrigerator until ready to use or peel and eat warm.

Nutrition: Calories: 77 Protein: 6.3 g Fiber: 0.0 g Net carbohydrates: 0.6 g Fat: 4.4 g Sodium: 62 mg Carbohydrates: 0.6 g Sugar: 0.6 g

Scrambled Eggs

Preparation Time: 5 minutes

Cooking Time: 15 minutes

Servings: 2

Ingredients:

- 4 large eggs
- 2 tablespoons unsalted butter, melted
- ½ cup shredded sharp Cheddar cheese

Directions:

1. Crack eggs into 2-cup round baking dish and whisk. Place dish into the air fryer basket.
2. Adjust the temperature to 400°F and set the timer for 10 minutes.
3. After 5 minutes, stir the eggs and add the butter and cheese. Let cook 3 more minutes and stir again.
4. Allow eggs to finish cooking an additional 2 minutes or remove if they are to your desired liking.
5. Use a fork to fluff. Serve warm.

Nutrition: Calories: 359 Protein: 19.5 g Fiber: 0.0 g Net carbohydrates: 1.1 g Fat: 27.6 g Sodium: 325 mg Carbohydrates: 1.1 g Sugar: 0.5 g

Loaded Cauliflower Breakfast Bake

Preparation Time: 15 minutes

Cooking Time: 20 minutes

Servings: 4

Ingredients:

- 6 large eggs
- ¼ cup heavy whipping cream
- 1½ cups chopped cauliflower
- 1 cup shredded medium Cheddar cheese
- 1 medium avocado, peeled and pitted
- 8 tablespoons full-fat sour cream
- 2 scallions, sliced on the bias
- 12 slices sugar-free bacon, cooked and crumbled

Directions:

1. In a medium bowl, whisk eggs and cream together. Pour into a 4-cup round baking dish.
2. Add cauliflower and mix, then top with Cheddar. Place dish into the air fryer basket.
3. Adjust the temperature to 320°F and set the timer for 20 minutes.
4. When completely cooked, eggs will be firm and cheese will be browned. Slice into four pieces.
5. Slice avocado and divide evenly among pieces. Top each piece with 2 tablespoons sour cream, sliced scallions, and crumbled bacon.

Nutrition: Calories: 512 Protein: 27.1 g Fiber: 3.2 g
Net carbohydrates: 4.3 g Fat: 38.3 g Sodium: 865 mg
Carbohydrates: 7.5 g Sugar: 2.3 g

Cinnamon Roll Sticks

Preparation Time: 10 minutes

Cooking Time: 7 minutes

Servings: 4 (2 sticks per serving)

Ingredients:

- 1 cup shredded mozzarella cheese
- 1 ounce full-fat cream cheese
- ⅓ cup blanched finely ground almond flour
- ½ teaspoon baking soda
- ½ cup granular erythritol, divided
- 1 teaspoon vanilla extract
- 1 large egg
- 2 tablespoons unsalted butter, melted
- ½ teaspoon ground cinnamon
- 3 tablespoons powdered erythritol
- 2 teaspoons unsweetened vanilla almond milk

Directions:

1. Place mozzarella in a large microwave-safe bowl and break cream cheese into small pieces and place into bowl. Microwave for 45 seconds.

2. Stir in almond flour, baking soda, ¼ cup granular erythritol, and vanilla. A soft dough should form. Microwave the mix for additional 15 seconds if it becomes too stiff.

3. Mix egg into the dough, using your hands if necessary.

4. Cut a piece of parchment to fit your air fryer basket. Press the dough into an 8" × 5" rectangle on the parchment and cut into eight (1") sticks.

5. In a small bowl, mix butter, cinnamon, and remaining granular erythritol. Brush half the mixture over the top of the sticks and place them into the air fryer basket.

6. Adjust the temperature to 400°F and set the timer for 7 minutes.

7. Halfway through the cooking time, flip the sticks and brush with remaining butter mixture. When done, sticks should be crispy.

8. To make glaze, whisk powdered erythritol and almond milk in a small bowl. Drizzle over cinnamon sticks. Serve warm.

Nutrition: Calories: 233 Protein: 10.3 g Fiber: 1.2 g Net carbohydrates: 2.2 g Sugar alcohol: 36.8 g Fat: 19.0 g Sodium: 378 mg Carbohydrates: 40.2 g Sugar: 1.0 g

Breakfast Calzone

Preparation Time: 15 minutes

Cooking Time: 15 minutes

Servings: 4

Ingredients:

- 1½ cups shredded mozzarella cheese
- ½ cup blanched finely ground almond flour
- 1 ounce full-fat cream cheese
- 1 large whole egg
- 4 large eggs, scrambled
- ½ pound cooked breakfast sausage, crumbled
- 8 tablespoons shredded mild Cheddar cheese

Directions:

1. In a large microwave-safe bowl, add mozzarella, almond flour, and cream cheese. Microwave for 1 minute. Stir until the mixture is smooth and forms a ball. Add the egg and stir until dough forms.

2. Place dough between two sheets of parchment and roll out to ¼" thickness. Cut the dough into four rectangles.

3. Mix scrambled eggs and cooked sausage together in a large bowl. Divide the mixture evenly among each piece of dough, placing it on the lower half

of the rectangle. Sprinkle each with 2 tablespoons Cheddar.

4. Fold over the rectangle to cover the egg and meat mixture. Pinch, roll, or use a wet fork to close the edges completely.
5. Cut a piece of parchment to fit your air fryer basket and place the calzones onto the parchment. Place parchment into the air fryer basket.
6. Adjust the temperature to 380°F and set the timer for 15 minutes.
7. Flip the calzones halfway through the cooking time. When done, calzones should be golden in color. Serve immediately.

Nutrition: Calories: 560 Protein: 34.5 g Fiber: 1.5 g Net carbohydrates: 4.2 g Fat: 41.7 g Sodium: 930 mg Carbohydrates: 5.7 g Sugar: 2.1 g

Cauliflower Avocado Toast

Preparation Time: 15 minutes

Cooking Time: 8 minutes

Servings: 2

Ingredients:

- 1 (12-ounce) steamer bag cauliflower
- 1 large egg
- ½ cup shredded mozzarella cheese
- 1 ripe medium avocado
- ½ teaspoon garlic powder
- ¼ teaspoon ground black pepper

Directions:

1. Cook cauliflower according to package instructions. Remove from bag and place into cheesecloth or clean towel to remove excess moisture.
2. Place cauliflower into a large bowl and mix in egg and mozzarella. Cut a piece of parchment to fit your air fryer basket. Separate the cauliflower mixture into two, and place it on the parchment in two mounds. Press out the cauliflower mounds into a ¼"-thick rectangle. Place the parchment into the air fryer basket.
3. Adjust the temperature to 400°F and set the timer for 8 minutes.
4. Flip the cauliflower halfway through the cooking time.

5. When the timer beeps, remove the parchment and allow the cauliflower to cool 5 minutes.
6. Cut open the avocado and remove the pit. Scoop out the inside, place it in a medium bowl, and mash it with garlic powder and pepper. Spread onto the cauliflower. Serve immediately.

Nutrition: Calories: 278 Protein: 14.1 g Fiber: 8.2 g Net carbohydrates: 7.7 g Fat: 15.6 g Sodium: 267 mg Carbohydrates: 15.9 g Sugar: 3.9 g

Sausage and Cheese Balls

Preparation Time: 10 minutes

Cooking Time: 12 minutes

Servings: 4

Ingredients:

- 1 pound pork breakfast sausage
- ½ cup shredded Cheddar cheese
- 1 ounce full-fat cream cheese, softened
- 1 large egg

Directions:

1. Mix all ingredients in a large bowl. Form into sixteen (1") balls. Place the balls into the air fryer basket.
2. Adjust the temperature to 400°F and set the timer for 12 minutes.
3. Shake the basket two- or three-times during cooking. Sausage balls will be browned on the outside and have an internal temperature of at least 145°F when completely cooked.
4. Serve warm.

Nutrition: Calories: 424 Protein: 22.8 g Fiber: 0.0 g Net carbohydrates: 1.6 g Fat: 32.2 g Sodium: 973 mg Carbohydrates: 1.6 g Sugar: 1.4 g

LUNCH

Parmesan Haddock Fillets

Preparation Time: 5 Minutes

Cooking Time: 11 to 13 Minutes

Servings: 2

Ingredients:

- ½ cup Parmesan cheese, freshly grated
- One teaspoon dried parsley flake
- One egg
- ¼ teaspoon cayenne pepper
- Two haddock fillets patted dry

Directions:

1. Warm the air fryer to 360ºF (182ºC).
2. Stir together the Parmesan cheese and parsley flakes in a shallow dish. Beat the egg with the cayenne pepper, sea salt, and pepper in a bowl.
3. Dunk the haddock fillets into the egg, and then roll over the Parmesan mixture until fully coated on both sides.
4. Handover the fillets to the air fryer basket and drizzle with the olive oil
5. Cook in the preheated air fryer for 11 to 13 minutes, or until the flesh is opaque.
6. Remove from the basket to a plate and serve.

Nutrition: Calories: 435 Fat: 26.4g Carbs: 4.4g Protein: 43.1g

Shrimp Skewers with Vermouth

Preparation Time: 10 Minutes

Cooking Time: 5 Minutes

Servings: 4

Ingredients:

- 1½ pounds (680 g) shrimp
- ¼ cup vermouth
- Two cloves garlic, crushed
- One lemon, cut into wedges

Directions:

1. Warm the air fryer to 400ºF (205ºC).
2. Toss the shrimp with the vermouth, olive oil, garlic, salt, and pepper in a bowl and then put it in the fridge to marinate for 1 hour.
3. Remove the shrimp from the refrigerator and discard the marinade. Skewer the shrimp by piercing through the center and transfer to the basket.
4. Cook in the warmed air fryer for 5 minutes, flipping the shrimp halfway through.
5. Relish with the lemon wedges and serve hot.

Nutrition: Calories: 229 Fat: 7.3g Carbs: 4.8g Protein: 25.3g

Lobster Tails with Green Olives

Preparation Time: 10 Minutes

Cooking Time: 7 Minutes

Servings: 5

Ingredients:

- 2 pounds (907 g) fresh lobster tails, cleaned and halved, in shells
- One teaspoon onion powder
- One teaspoon cayenne pepper
- Two garlic cloves, minced
- 1 cup of green olives

Directions:

1. Warm the air fryer to 390ºF (199ºC) and spray the basket with cooking spray.
2. Put all the ingredients except for the green olives in a sealable plastic bag. Seal the bag and shake until the lobster tails are coated completely.
3. Arrange the coated lobster tails in the greased basket. Cook in batches in the preheated air fryer for 6 to 7 minutes, shaking the basket halfway through.
4. Remove from the basket and serve with green olives.

Nutrition: Calories: 188 Fat: 6.8g Carbs: 1.9g Protein: 30.3g

Grilled Sardines

Preparation Time: 5 Minutes

Cooking Time: 21 Minutes

Servings: 2

Ingredients:

- Five sardines
- Herbs of Provence

Directions:

1. Preheat the air fryer to 1600C.
2. Spray the basket and place your sardines in the basket of your fryer.
3. Set the timer for 14 minutes. After 7 minutes, remember to turn the sardines so that they are roasted on both sides.

Nutrition: Calories 189g Fat 10g Carbohydrates 0g Sugars 0g Protein 22g Cholesterol 128mg

Zucchini with Tuna

Preparation Time: 10-20 Minutes

Cooking Time: 15-30 Minutes

Servings: 2

Ingredients:

- Four medium zucchinis
- 120g of tuna in oil (canned) drained
- 30g grated cheese
- tsp pine nuts
- Salt, pepper to taste

Directions:

1. Cut the zucchini in half lengthways and empty it with a small spoon (set aside the pulp that will be used for the filling); place them in the basket.
2. In a food processor, put the zucchini pulp, drained tuna, pine nuts, and grated cheese. Blend everything until you get a homogeneous and dense mixture.
3. Fill the zucchini. Set the air fryer to 1800C.
4. Simmer for 20 min. Depending on the size of the zucchini. Let cool before serving

Nutrition: Calories 389 Carbohydrates 10g Fat 29g Sugars 5g Protein 23g Cholesterol 40mg

Caramelized Salmon Fillet

Preparation Time: 10 Minutes

Cooking Time: 30 Minutes

Servings: 4

Ingredients:

- Two salmon fillets
- 60g cane sugar
- 4 tbsp soy sauce
- 50g sesame seeds
- Unlimited Ginger

Directions:

1. Preheat the air fryer at 1800C for 5 minutes.
2. Put the sugar and soy sauce in the basket.
3. Cook everything for 5 minutes.
4. In the meantime, wash the fish well, pass it through sesame to cover it completely, and place it inside the tank and add the fresh ginger.
5. Cook for 12 minutes.
6. Turn the fish over and finish cooking for another 8 minutes.

Nutrition: Calories 569 Fat 14.9 g Carbohydrates 40 g Sugars 27.6 g Protein 66.9 g Cholesterol 165.3 mg

Breaded Swordfish

Preparation Time: 20 Minutes

Cooking Time: 30 Minutes

Servings: 8

Ingredients:

- 500g swordfish ranches
- Breadcrumbs to taste
- 1 tsp peanut oil
- 1 tsp olive oil
- ½ lemon juice

Directions:

1. Clean and rinse the fish; grease each slice and pass it in lightly salted breadcrumbs to cover it completely.
2. Preheat the air fryer at 1600C for 5 minutes.
3. Place the breaded fish in the basket—Cook the fish for 10 minutes.
4. Turn the fish over and cook for additional 8 minutes.
5. Meanwhile, prepare the marinade with olive oil, lemon juice, salt, pepper, and chopped parsley; mix with a fork.
6. Once ready, place the fish slices on the plate and pour 1 to 2 tablespoons of marinade.

Nutrition: Calories 67 Fat 3.79g Carbohydrates 2.23g Sugars 0.22g Protein 5.67g Cholesterol 16mg

Deep Fried Prawns

Preparation Time: 20 Minutes

Cooking Time: 15 Minutes

Servings: 6

Ingredients:

- 12 prawns
- Two eggs
- Flour to taste
- Breadcrumbs
- 1 tsp oil

Directions:

1. Remove the head of the prawns and shell carefully.
2. Pass the prawns first in the flour, then in the beaten egg, and then in the breadcrumbs.
3. Preheat the air fryer for 1 minute at 1500C.
4. Add the prawns and cook for 4 minutes. If the prawns are large, it will be necessary to cook six at a time.
5. Turn the prawns and cook for another 4 minutes.
6. They should be served with a yogurt or mayonnaise sauce.

Nutrition: Calories 2385.1 Fat 23 Carbohydrates 52.3g Sugar 0.1g Protein 21.4g

Mussels with Pepper

Preparation Time: 20 Minutes

Cooking Time: 15 Minutes

Servings: 6

Ingredients:

- 700g mussels
- One clove garlic
- 1 tsp oil
- Pepper to taste
- Parsley Taste

Directions:

1. Clean and scrape the mold cover and remove the byssus (the "beard" that comes out of the mold).
2. Pour the oil, clean the mussels, and the crushed garlic in the basket.
3. Set the temperature to 2000C and simmer for 12 minutes.
4. Towards the end of cooking, add black pepper and chopped parsley.
5. Finally, distribute the mussel juice well at the bottom of the basket, stirring the basket.

Nutrition: Calories 150 Carbohydrates 2g Fat 8g Sugars 0g Protein 15g Cholesterol 0mg

Scallops in Butter with Leaves

Preparation Time: 20 Minutes

Cooking Time: 30 Minutes

Servings: 4

Ingredients:

- 400g scallops
- 20g butter
- One clove garlic
- Leaves to taste
- ½ lemon juice

Directions:

1. Wash the scallops and dry them on a paper towel.
2. Place the butter and chopped garlic inside the basket. Set the temperature to 1500C.
3. Melt the butter for 2 to 3 minutes.
4. Add the scallops, salt, pepper, and cook for 8 minutes.
5. Then add the lemon juice, parsley, and finish cooking for another 3 to 4 minutes.
6. Very good as an appetizer to serve inside the shells.

Nutrition: Calories 315.6 Fat 13.8 g Carbohydrate 11.0 g Sugars 0.1 g Protein38.7 g Cholesterol 114.8 mg

DINNER

Italian Baked Egg and Veggies

Preparation time: 10 minutes

Cooking time: 10 minutes

Servings: 2

Ingredients:

- 2 tablespoons salted butter
- 1 small zucchini, sliced lengthwise and quartered
- ½ medium green bell pepper, seeded and diced
- 1 cup fresh spinach, chopped
- 1 medium Roma tomato, diced
- 2 large eggs
- ¼ teaspoon onion powder
- ¼ teaspoon garlic powder
- ½ teaspoon dried basil
- ¼ teaspoon dried oregano

Directions:

1. Grease two (4") ramekins with 1 tablespoon butter each.
2. In a large bowl, toss zucchini, bell pepper, spinach, and tomatoes. Divide the mixture in two and place half in each ramekin.
3. Crack an egg on top of each ramekin and sprinkle with onion powder, garlic powder, basil, and oregano. Place into the air fryer basket.
4. Adjust the temperature to 330°F and set the timer for 10 minutes.
5. Serve immediately.

Nutrition: Calories: 150 Protein: 8.3 g Fiber: 2.2 g Net carbohydrates: 4.4 g Fat: 10.0 g Sodium: 135 mg Carbohydrates: 6.6 g Sugar: 3.7 g

BBQ "Pulled" Mushrooms

Preparation time: 5 minutes

Cooking time: 12 minutes

Servings: 2

Ingredients:

- 4 large portobello mushrooms
- 1 tablespoon salted butter, melted
- ¼ teaspoon ground black pepper
- 1 teaspoon chili powder
- 1 teaspoon paprika
- ¼ teaspoon onion powder
- ½ cup low-carb, sugar-free barbecue sauce

Directions:

1. Remove stem and scoop out the underside of each mushroom. Brush the caps with butter and sprinkle with pepper, chili powder, paprika, and onion powder.
2. Place mushrooms into the air fryer basket.
3. Adjust the temperature to 400°F and set the timer for 8 minutes.
4. When the timer beeps, remove mushrooms from the basket and place on a cutting board or work surface. Using two forks, gently pull the mushrooms apart, creating strands.

5. Place mushroom strands into a 4-cup round baking dish with barbecue sauce. Place dish into the air fryer basket.
6. Adjust the temperature to 350°F and set the timer for 4 minutes.
7. Stir halfway through the cooking time. Serve warm.

Nutrition: Calories: 108 Protein: 3.3 g Fiber: 2.7 g Net carbohydrates: 8.2 g Fat: 5.9 g Sodium: 476 mg Carbohydrates: 10.9 g Sugar: 3.6 g

Lemon Garlic Shrimp

Preparation time: 5 minutes

Cooking time: 6 minutes

Servings: 2

Ingredients:

- 1 medium lemon
- 8 ounces medium shelled and deveined shrimp
- 2 tablespoons unsalted butter, melted
- ½ teaspoon Old Bay seasoning
- ½ teaspoon minced garlic

Directions:

1. Zest lemon and then cut in half. Place shrimp in a large bowl and squeeze juice from ½ lemon on top of them.
2. Add lemon zest to bowl along with remaining ingredients. Toss shrimp until fully coated.
3. Pour bowl contents into 6" round baking dish. Place into the air fryer basket.
4. Adjust the temperature to 400°F and set the timer for 6 minutes.
5. Shrimp will be bright pink when fully cooked. Serve warm with pan sauce.

Nutrition: Calories: 190 Protein: 16.4 g Fiber: 0.4 g Net carbohydrates: 2.5 g Fat: 11.8 g Sodium: 812 mg Carbohydrates: 2.9 g Sugar: 0.5 g

Cajun Salmon

Preparation time: 5 minutes

Cooking time: 7 minutes

Servings: 2

Ingredients:

- 2 (4-ounce) salmon fillets, skin removed
- 2 tablespoons unsalted butter, melted
- ⅛ teaspoon ground cayenne pepper
- ½ teaspoon garlic powder
- 1 teaspoon paprika
- ¼ teaspoon ground black pepper

Directions:

1. Brush each fillet with butter.
2. Combine remaining ingredients in a small bowl and then rub onto fish. Place fillets into the air fryer basket.
3. Adjust the temperature to 390°F and set the timer for 7 minutes.
4. When fully cooked, internal temperature will be 145°F. Serve immediately.

Nutrition: Calories: 253 Protein: 20.9 g Fiber: 0.4 g Net carbohydrates: 1.0 g Fat: 16.6 g Sodium: 46 mg Carbohydrates: 1.4 g Sugar: 0.1 g

Blackened Shrimp

Preparation time: 5 minutes

Cooking time: 6 minutes

Servings: 2

Ingredients:

- 8 ounces medium shelled and deveined shrimp
- 2 tablespoons salted butter, melted
- 1 teaspoon paprika
- ½ teaspoon garlic powder
- ¼ teaspoon onion powder
- ½ teaspoon Old Bay seasoning

Directions:

1. Toss all ingredients together in a large bowl. Place shrimp into the air fryer basket.
2. Adjust the temperature to 400°F and set the timer for 6 minutes.
3. Turn the shrimp halfway through the cooking time to ensure even cooking. Serve immediately.

Nutrition: Calories: 192 Protein: 16.6 g Fiber: 0.5 g Net carbohydrates: 2.0 g Fat: 11.9 g Sodium: 902 mg Carbohydrates: 2.5 g Sugar: 0.2 g

Coconut Shrimp

Preparation time: 5 minutes

Cooking time: 6 minutes

Servings: 2

Ingredients:

- 8 ounces medium shelled and deveined shrimp
- 2 tablespoons salted butter, melted
- ½ teaspoon Old Bay seasoning
- ¼ cup unsweetened shredded coconut

Directions:

1. In a large bowl, toss the shrimp in butter and Old Bay seasoning.
2. Place shredded coconut in bowl. Coat each piece of shrimp in the coconut and place into the air fryer basket.
3. Adjust the temperature to 400°F and set the timer for 6 minutes.
4. Gently turn the shrimp halfway through the cooking time. Serve immediately.

Nutrition: Calories: 252 Protein: 16.9 G Fiber: 2.0 G Net Carbohydrates: 1.8 G Fat: 17.8 G Sodium: 902 Mg Carbohydrates: 3.8 G Sugar: 0.7 G

Foil-Packet Salmon

Preparation time: 10 minutes

Cooking time: 12 minutes

Servings: 2

Ingredients:

- 2 (4-ounce) salmon fillets, skin removed
- 2 tablespoons unsalted butter, melted
- ½ teaspoon garlic powder
- 1 medium lemon
- ½ teaspoon dried dill

Directions:

1. Place each fillet on a 5" × 5" square of aluminum foil. Drizzle with butter and sprinkle with garlic powder.
2. Zest half of the lemon and sprinkle zest over salmon. Slice other half of the lemon and lay two slices on each piece of salmon. Sprinkle dill over salmon.
3. Gather and fold foil at the top and sides to fully close packets. Place foil packets into the air fryer basket.
4. Adjust the temperature to 400°F and set the timer for 12 minutes.
5. Salmon will be easily flaked and have an internal temperature of at least 145°F when fully cooked. Serve immediately.

Nutrition: Calories: 252 Protein: 20.9 g Fiber: 0.4 g
Net carbohydrates: 0.8 g Fat: 16.5 g Sodium: 47 mg
Carbohydrates: 1.2 g Sugar: 0.2 g

Salmon Patties

Preparation time: 10 minutes

Cooking time: 8 minutes

Servings: 2

Ingredients:

- 2 (5-ounce) pouches cooked pink salmon
- 1 large egg
- ¼ cup ground pork rinds
- 2 tablespoons full-fat mayonnaise
- 2 teaspoons sriracha
- 1 teaspoon chili powder

Directions:

1. mix all ingredients in a large bowl and form into four patties. Place patties into the air fryer basket.
2. adjust the temperature to 400°f and set the timer for 8 minutes.
3. carefully flip each patty halfway through the cooking time. Patties will be crispy on the outside when fully cooked.

Nutrition: Calories: 319 Protein: 33.8 g Fiber: 0.5 g Net carbohydrates: 1.4 g Fat: 19.0 g Sodium: 843 mg Carbohydrates: 1.9 g Sugar: 1.3 g

Firecracker Shrimp

Preparation time: 10 minutes

Cooking time: 7 minutes

Servings: 4

Ingredients:

- 1 pound medium shelled and deveined shrimp
- 2 tablespoons salted butter, melted
- ½ teaspoon Old Bay seasoning
- ¼ teaspoon garlic powder
- 2 tablespoons sriracha
- ¼ teaspoon powdered erythritol
- ¼ cup full-fat mayonnaise
- ⅛ teaspoon ground black pepper

Directions:

1. In a large bowl, toss shrimp in butter, Old Bay seasoning, and garlic powder. Place shrimp into the air fryer basket.
2. Adjust the temperature to 400°F and set the timer for 7 minutes.
3. Flip the shrimp halfway through the cooking time. Shrimp will be bright pink when fully cooked.
4. In another large bowl, mix sriracha, powdered erythritol, mayonnaise, and pepper. Toss shrimp in the spicy mixture and serve immediately.

Nutrition: Calories: 143 Protein: 16.4 g Fiber: 0.0 g
Net carbohydrates: 2.8 g Sugar alcohol: 0.2 g Fat: 6.4
g
Sodium: 936 mg Carbohydrates: 3.0 g Sugar: 1.5 g

Crab Legs

Preparation time: 5 minutes

Cooking time: 15 minutes

Servings: 4

Ingredients:

- ¼ cup salted butter, melted and divided
- 3 pounds crab legs
- ¼ teaspoon garlic powder
- Juice of ½ medium lemon

Directions:

1. In a large bowl, drizzle 2 tablespoons butter over crab legs. Place crab legs into the air fryer basket.
2. Adjust the temperature to 400°F and set the timer for 15 minutes.
3. Shake the air fryer basket to toss the crab legs halfway through the cooking time.
4. In a small bowl, mix remaining butter, garlic powder, and lemon juice.
5. To serve, crack open crab legs and remove meat. Dip in lemon butter.

Nutrition: Calories: 123 Protein: 15.7 g Fiber: 0.0 g Net carbohydrates: 0.4 g Fat: 5.6 g Sodium: 756 mg Carbohydrates: 0.4 g Sugar: 0.1 g

SIDES

Roasted Corn

Preparation Time: 5 Minutes

Cooking Time: 10 Minutes

Servings: 4

Ingredients:

- Four fresh ears of corn
- Two teaspoons olive oil
- salt and pepper to taste

Directions:

1. Remove the corn husks and wash and pat dry the cob.
2. If you need to, cut down the cob to fit in your basket.
3. Drizzle a little oil over each cob and sprinkle with salt and pepper.
4. Cook at 400 degrees for 10 minutes.

Nutrition: Calories: 100 Sodium: 0 mg Dietary Fiber:1 g Fat: 2.8 g Carbs: 16 g Protein: 2 g

Seasoned Potato Wedges

Preparation Time: 10 Minutes

Cooking Time: 20 Minutes

Servings: 4

Ingredients:

- Four russet potatoes
- One tablespoon bacon fat
- One teaspoon paprika
- One teaspoon chili powder
- One teaspoon salt

Directions

1. Wash potatoes and portion into eight slices.
2. Warm bacon fat in the microwave for 10 seconds.
3. Combine all of your dry seasonings in a bowl and toss to mix.
4. Add bacon fat to the bowl and stir.
5. Toss the wedges in the bowl and transfer to the basket.
6. Cook at the preset chicken setting, tossing halfway through.

Nutrition: Calories:171 Sodium: 684 mg Dietary Fiber:5.6g Fat: 1.9g Carbs: 34.3g Protein: 5.1g

Honey Roasted Carrots

Preparation Time: 5 Minutes

Cooking Time: 10 Minutes

Servings: 4

Ingredients:

- One tablespoon olive oil
- 3 cups baby carrots
- One tablespoon honey
- salt and pepper to taste

Directions:

1. In a container, put the carrots, then using oil and honey, drizzle it.
2. Sprinkle on salt and pepper, then using a wooden spoon, blend it entirely.
3. Position the carrots in the basket, then cook at 400 degrees for 10 minutes.
4. For best results, serve immediately.

Nutrition: Calories:83 Sodium: 74 mg Dietary Fiber:2.5g Fat: 3.5g Carbs: 13g Protein: 1.3g

Home Made Tater Tots

Preparation Time: 40 Minutes

Cooking Time: 20 Minutes

Servings: 3

Ingredients:

- Three russet potatoes
- Two tablespoons dehydrated chopped onion
- Two tablespoons corn starch
- One tablespoon chive
- One teaspoon garlic powder

Directions:

1. Scrub the potatoes and peel them.
2. Mince the chives.
3. Combine two tablespoons of hot water and the dehydrated onions in a bowl and set aside.
4. Grate the potatoes into a bowl and fill with cold water.
5. Strain the potatoes and repeat the process to get rid of extra starch.
6. Add corn starch to the potatoes and mix well to combine.
7. Preheat your oven to 400 degrees.
8. Spread the potatoes outdone a baking sheet and bake for 20 minutes

9. Allow the potatoes to cool, then transfer them to a bowl and mix well with all other ingredients.

10. Scoop out 1 – 2 tablespoons of the mixture and place them in your basket.

11. Cook at 350 degrees for 20 minutes, shaking a few times during the cooking process.

Nutrition: Calories:177 Sodium: 13 mg Dietary Fiber:5.3g Fat: 0.2g Carbs: 40.9g Protein: 4g

Roasted Brussels Sprouts

Preparation Time: 5 Minutes

Cooking Time: 15 Minutes

Servings: 4

Ingredients:

- 1-pound fresh brussels sprouts
- Five teaspoons olive oil
- 1/2 teaspoon kosher salt

Directions:

1. Toss all of the fixings together in a bowl.
2. Choose the French Fry preset.
3. Pull the basket out slightly and shake the ingredients a few times during cooking.

Nutrition: Calories:99 Sodium: 319 mg Dietary Fiber:4.3g Fat: 6.2g Carbs: 10.3g Protein: 3.9g

Baked Sweet Potato

Preparation Time: 5 Minutes

Cooking Time: 40 Minutes

Servings: 3

Ingredients:

- Three sweet potatoes
- One tablespoon olive oil
- salt to taste

Directions:

1. Wash sweet potatoes and pat dry.
2. Brush the potatoes with olive oil and sprinkling with salt.
3. Preheat the air fryer to 400 degrees.
4. Set the timer at 30 minutes and flip at the 20-minute mark. When the timer goes off, reset it for another 10 minutes to finish cooking.

Nutrition: Calories: 170 Sodium: 45 mg Dietary Fiber: 4 g Fat: 4.7 g Carbs: 33 g Protein: 2 g

Vermouth Roasted Mushrooms

Preparation Time: 10 Minutes

Cooking Time: 25 Minutes

Servings: 4

Ingredients:

- 2 pounds button mushrooms
- tablespoon duck fat
- 1/2 teaspoon garlic powder
- Two teaspoons herb de Provence
- Two tablespoons white vermouth

Directions:

1. Wash the mushrooms and spin dry.
2. Warm up the duck fat, garlic powder, vermouth, and herbs in a skillet for 5 minutes, mixing well.
3. Toss the mushrooms in the skillet and transfer to the basket.
4. Cook at 320 degrees for 25 minutes, tossing once at the 15-minute mark.

Nutrition: Calories:86 Sodium: 13 mg Dietary Fiber:2.3 g Fat: 3.8 g Carbs: 7.9 g Protein: 7.2 g

Lemony Green Beans

Preparation Time: 5 Minutes

Cooking Time: 10 Minutes

Servings: 4

Ingredients:

- 1-pound fresh green beans
- One lemon
- salt and pepper to taste
- 1/4 teaspoon olive oil

Directions:

1. Wash and destem the green beans.
2. Put the beans in a container and sprinkle oil over the top of them.
3. Cut the lemon in half and squeeze fresh lemon juice over the beans.
4. Season with salt and pepper and pitch well.
5. Transfer the beans to your basket and cook at 400 degrees for 10 minutes.

Nutrition: Calories:42 Sodium: 7 mg Dietary Fiber:4.3 g Fat: 0.5 g Carbs: 9.4 g Protein: 2.2 g

Air Fryer Bread Sticks

Preparation Time: 10 Minutes

Cooking Time: 12 Minutes

Servings: 12

Ingredients:

- One can prepared pizza crust
- One tablespoon butter
- 1/2 cup shredded provolone cheese
- One tablespoon parmesan cheese
- One tablespoon basil

Directions:

1. Melt the butter.
2. Unroll the pizza crust onto a flat surface and brush with butter.
3. Sprinkle the cheese, spices, and salt evenly over the dough.
4. Cut the dough in half parallel, then cut each half vertically into 12 pieces each.
5. Preheat the fryer to 400 degrees.
6. Working in small batches and giving the breadsticks room, cook for 12 minutes, flipping the sticks at the 10-minute mark.

Nutrition: Calories:43 Sodium: 101 mg Dietary Fiber:0.1 g Fat: 2.7 g Carbs: 2.8 g Protein: 2g

Potato Chips

Preparation Time: 5 Minutes

Cooking Time: 30 Minutes

Servings: 3

Ingredients:

- Three russet potatoes
- 1/2 teaspoon olive oil
- sea salt to taste

Directions:

1. Scrub potatoes and pat dry.
2. Leave the skin on and cut potatoes into thin slices.
3. Toss the potato slices in oil and sea salt.
4. Preheat fryer to 400 degrees.
5. Cook for 30 minutes, tossing ingredients often.

Nutrition: Calories:164 Sodium: 469 mg Dietary Fiber:3.2 g Fat: 5.3 g Carbs: 20.8 g Protein: 10.2g

DESSERTS

Air Fryer Oven Soft Chocolate Brownies

Preparation Time: 5 minutes

Cooking Time: 14 minutes

Servings: 2

Ingredients:

- 2 tsp. vanilla essence 12g caster sugar
- 100g Self Raising flour 2 tbsp. water
- Two medium eggs (beaten) 142ml
- 175g brown sugar50g chocolate
- 125g butter

Directions:

1. Preheat air fryer oven to 180C
2. Melt butter and chocolate in a bowl above the pan over medium heat. Add brown sugar, medium egg and vanilla essence, then ad self-rising flour and mix properly
3. Pour mixture into a greased dish that can be contained in an air fryer oven
4. Cook in air fryer oven at 180C for 15 minutes

5. While the brownie is cooking, mix caster sugar and water in a pan over medium heat until sugar is melted. Turn up the heat and cook for 3 minutes until color turns light brown, then take off and rest for 2 minutes
6. Add butter to sugar liquid until melted, and slowly add the milk. Set aside to cool
7. When brownies are ready, chop into squares, place on the plate alongside sliced bananas and cover with caramel sauce. Serve

Nutrition: Calories 238 Fat 6g Protein 1g Sugar 4g

Air Fryer Oven Chocolate Éclairs

Preparation Time: 5 minutes

Cooking Time: 35 minutes

Servings: 6

Ingredients:

- Éclair dough
- 150ml water50g butter
- Three medium eggs
- 100g plain flour
- Cream filling
- 1 tsp. icing sugar1 tsp. vanilla essence
- 150ml whipped cream
- Chocolate topping
- 25g butter1 tbsp. whipped cream
- 50g milk chocolate (chopped into chunks)

Directions:

1. Preheat air fryer oven to 180C
2. Place fat in water and heat over medium heat. Remove from heat and stir in flour, then return to heat and stir until it forms a medium ball in the middle of the pan
3. Transfer to plate to cool then beat in eggs until mixture is smooth then make into éclair shapes
4. Place in air fryer oven and cook at 180C for 10 minutes then on 160C for 8 minutes

5. While the dough is cooking, mix vanilla essence with whipped cream and icing sugar until nice and thick

6. While éclairs are ready and cooling, make the chocolate topping by placing milk chocolate, butter and whipped cream in a glass bowl. Place the bowl over a pan of hot water and mix well until chocolate melts

7. Cover éclairs with melted chocolate and serve

Nutrition: Calories 471 Fat 24g Protein 4.1g Sugar 6g

Vanilla Soufflé

Preparation Time: 5 minutes

Cooking Time: 5 minutes

Servings: 16

Ingredients:

- ¼ cup All-Purpose Flour ¼ cup Butter (softened)
- 1 cup Whole Milk ¼ cup Sugar 4
- Egg Yolks 2 tsp. Vanilla Extract
- 1 Vanilla Bean 5 Egg Whites
- 1 oz. Sugar 1 tsp. Cream of Tartar

Directions:

1. Mix the flour and butter to smooth paste.
2. Heat milk and dissolve the sugar in a pan and bring to a boil.
3. Add the flour and butter mixture to the boiling milk, whisk hard to ensure smoothness.
4. Simmer for several minutes until the mix thickens, then cool in the ice bath for 10 minutes
5. Take six 3-ounce soufflé dishes, coat with butter and sugar (not mixed with the ingredients).
6. In another mixing bowl, quickly beat the egg yolks and vanilla extract and add to the cooling milk mixture.
7. Beat the egg whites, sugar, and cream of tartar until the egg whites form medium-stiff peaks.

8. Fold the egg whites into the soufflé base and pour into the prepared baking dishes.
9. Preheat the Air fryer oven to 320°F, place three soufflé dishes and cook for 12-15 minutes.
10.   Serve with a sprinkle of powdered sugar and chocolate Auglaize sauce.

Nutrition: Calories 303 Fat 3g Protein 0.5g Sugar 4g

Banana Split

Preparation Time: 15 minutes

Cooking Time: 14 minutes

Servings: 8

Ingredients:

- 3 tbsp. coconut oil
- 1 cup panko breadcrumbs
- ½ cup of corn flour
- Two eggs
- Four bananas, peeled and halved lengthwise
- 3 tbsp. sugar
- ¼ tsp. ground cinnamon
- 2 tbsp. walnuts, chopped

Directions

1. In a medium skillet, melt the coconut oil over medium heat and cook breadcrumbs for about 3-4 minutes or until golden browned and crumbled, stirring continuously.
2. Transfer the breadcrumbs into a shallow bowl and set aside to cool.
3. In a second bowl, place the corn flour.
4. In a third bowl, whisk the eggs.
5. Coat the banana slices with flour, dip into eggs, and finally, coat evenly with the breadcrumbs.
6. In a prepared small bowl, mix the sugar and cinnamon.

7. Press "Power Button" of Air Fry Oven and turn the dial to select the "Air Fry" mode.

8. Set the cooking time to 10 minutes.

9. Now push the Temp button and rotate the dial to set the temperature at 280 degrees F.

10. Press the "Start/Pause" button to start.

11. When the unit beeps it means that it is preheated, open the lid.

12. Arrange the banana slices in "Air Fry Basket" and sprinkle them with cinnamon sugar.

13. Insert the basket in the oven.

14. Transfer the banana slices onto plates to cool slightly

15. Sprinkle with chopped walnuts and serve.

Nutrition: Calories 216 Total Fat 8.8g Sodium 16 mg Total Carbs 26 g Fiber 2.3 g Protein 3.4 g

Crispy Banana Slices

Preparation Time: 15 minutes

Cooking Time: 15 minutes

Servings: 8

Ingredients:

- Four medium ripe bananas, peeled
- 1/3 cup rice flour, divided
- 2 tbsp. all-purpose flour

- 2 tbsp. corn flour
- 2 tbsp. desiccated coconut
- ½ tsp. baking powder
- ½ tsp. ground cardamom
- Pinch of salt
- Water, as required
- ¼ cup sesame seeds

Directions

1. In a shallow bowl, mix 2 tbsp. of rice flour, all-purpose flour, corn flour, coconut, baking powder, cardamom, and salt.
2. Gradually, add the water and mix until a thick and smooth mixture forms.
3. In a second bowl, place the remaining rice flour.
4. In a third bowl, add the sesame seeds.
5. Cut each banana into half and then cut each half into two pieces lengthwise.
6. Dip the banana slices into the coconut mixture and then coat with the remaining rice flour, followed by the sesame seeds.
7. Press "Power Button" of Air Fry Oven and turn the dial to select the "Air Fry" mode.
8. Set the cooking time to 15 minutes.
9. Now push the Temp button and rotate the dial to set the temperature at 390 degrees F.
10. Press the "Start/Pause" button to start.

---

11. When the unit beeps it means that it is preheated, open the lid.

12. Arrange the banana slices in "Air Fry Basket" and insert them in the oven.

13. Transfer the banana slices onto plates to cool slightly

14. Transfer the banana slices onto plates to cool slightly before serving.

Nutrition: Calories 121 Total Fat 3 g Sodium 21 mg Total Carbs 23.1 g Fiber 2.6 g Protein 2.2 g

Pineapple Bites

Preparation Time: 10 minutes

Cooking Time: 10 minutes

Servings: 4

Ingredients:

- For Pineapple Sticks:
- ½ of pineapple
- ¼ cup desiccated coconut
- For Yogurt Dip:
- 1 tbsp. fresh mint leaves, minced
- 1 cup vanilla yogurt

Directions

1. Remove the outer skin of the pineapple and cut into long 1-2-inch-thick sticks.
2. In a shallow dish, place the coconut.
3. Coat the pineapple sticks with coconut evenly.
4. Press "Power Button" of Air Fry Oven and turn the dial to select the "Air Fry" mode.
5. Set the cooking time to 10 minutes.
6. Now push the Temp button and rotate the dial to set the temperature at 390 degrees F.
7. Press the "Start/Pause" button to start.
8. When the unit beeps it means that it is preheated, open the lid.
9. Arrange the pineapple sticks in a lightly greased "Air Fry Basket" and insert them in the oven.

10.   Meanwhile, for a dip in a bowl, mix mint and yogurt.

11.   Serve pineapple sticks with yogurt dip.

Nutrition: Calories 124 Total Fat 2.6 g Cholesterol 4 mg Total Carbs 21.6 g Fiber 2.3 g Protein 4.4 g

Cheesecake Bites

Preparation Time: 20 minutes

Cooking Time: 2 minutes

Servings: 12

Ingredients:

- 8 oz. cream cheese, softened
- ½ cup plus 2 tbsps. sugar, divided
- 4 tbsp. heavy cream, divided
- ½ tsp. vanilla extract
- ½ cup almond flour

Directions

1. In a stand mixer bowl, fitted with the paddle attachment, add the cream cheese, ½ cup of sugar, 2 tbsp. of heavy cream and vanilla extract and beat until smooth.
2. With a scooper, scoop the mixture onto a parchment paper-lined baking pan.
3. Freeze for about 30 minutes or until firm.
4. In a prepared small bowl, place the remaining cream.
5. In another small bowl, add the almond flour and remaining sugar and mix well.
6. Dip each cheesecake bite in cream and then coat with the flour mixture.

7. Press "Power Button" of Air Fry Oven and turn the dial to select the "Air Fry" mode.

8. Set the cooking time to 2 minutes.

9. Now push the Temp button and rotate the dial to set the temperature at 300 degrees F.

10. Press the "Start/Pause" button to start.

11. When the unit beeps it means that it is preheated, open the lid.

12. Arrange the pan in "Air Fry Basket" and insert it in the oven.

13. Serve warm.

Nutrition: Calories 149 Fat 10.7 g Cholesterol 28 mg Carbs 11.7 g Fiber 0.5 g Protein 2.5 g

Chocolate Bites

Preparation Time: 15 minutes

Cooking Time: 13 minutes

Servings: 8

Ingredients:

- 2 cups plain flour
- 2 tbsp. cocoa powder
- ½ cup icing sugar
- Pinch of ground cinnamon
- 1 tsp. vanilla extract
- ¾ cup chilled butter
- ¼ cup chocolate, chopped into 8 chunks

Directions

1. In a bowl, mix the flour, icing sugar, cocoa powder, cinnamon and vanilla extract.
2. With a pastry cutter, cut the butter and mix till a smooth dough form.
3. Divide the dough into eight equal-sized balls.
4. Press one chocolate chunk in the center of each ball and cover with the dough thoroughly.
5. Place the balls into the baking pan.
6. Press "Power Button" of Air Fry Oven and turn the dial to select the "Air Fry" mode.
7. Set the cooking time to 8 minutes.
8. Now push the Temp button and rotate the dial to set the temperature at 355 degrees F.
9. Press the "Start/Pause" button to start.

10.   When the unit beeps it means that it is preheated, open the lid.

11.   Arrange the pan in "Air Fry Basket" and insert it in the oven.

12.   After 8 minutes of cooking, set the temperature at 320 degrees F for 5 minutes.

13.   Place the baking pan onto the wire rack to cool completely before serving.

Nutrition: Calories 328 Fat 19.3 g Sodium 128 mg Carbs 35.3 g Protein 4.1 g

Shortbread Fingers

Preparation Time: 15 minutes

Cooking Time: 12 minutes

Servings: 10

Ingredients:
- 1/3 cup caster sugar
- 1 2/3 cups plain flour
- ¾ cup butter

Directions
1. In a large bowl, mix the sugar and flour.
2. Add the butter and mix until a smooth dough form.
3. Cut the dough into ten equal-sized fingers.
4. With a fork, lightly prick the fingers.

5. Place the fingers into the lightly greased baking pan.
6. Press "Power Button" of Air Fry Oven and turn the dial to select the "Air Fry" mode.
7. Set the cooking time to 12 minutes.
8. Now push the Temp button and rotate the dial to set the temperature at 355 degrees F.
9. Press the "Start/Pause" button to start.
10. When the unit beeps it means that it is preheated, open the lid.
11. Arrange the pan in "Air Fry Basket" and insert it in the oven.
12. Place the baking pan onto a wire rack to cool for about 5-10 minutes.
13. Now, invert the shortbread fingers onto a wire rack to completely cool before serving.

Nutrition: Calories 223 Total Fat 14 g Cholesterol 37 mg Sodium 99 mg Total Carbs 22.6 g Fiber 0.6 g Protein 2.3 g

Berry Tacos

Preparation Time: 15 minutes

Cooking Time: 5 minutes

Servings: 2

Ingredients:

- 2 soft shell tortillas
- 4 tbsp. strawberry jelly
- ¼ cup fresh blueberries
- ¼ cup fresh raspberries
- 2 tbsp. powdered sugar

Directions

1. Spread 2 tbsp. of strawberry jelly over each tortilla
2. Top each with berries evenly and sprinkle with powdered sugar.
3. Press "Power Button" of Air Fry Oven and turn the dial to select the "Air Fry" mode.
4. Set the cooking time to 5 minutes.
5. Now push the Temp button and rotate the dial to set the temperature at 300 degrees F.
6. Press the "Start/Pause" button to start.
7. When the unit beeps it means that it is preheated, open the lid.
8. Arrange the tortillas in "Air Fry Basket" and insert them in the oven.
9. Serve warm.

Nutrition: Calories 216 Total Fat 0.8 g Sodium 11 mg
Total Carbs 53.2 g Fiber 3 g Protein 1.7 g

CONCLUSION

Here are some of the frequently asked questions about air fryers that might help you.

What Foods are Suitable to be cooked in an Air Fryer?

As the name implies, Air Fryer was programmed to suite foods that can be baked. roasted fried, and grilled. Foods cooked in the Air Fryer are always delicious and crispy. Foods that required light flour coating, mainly for frying are suited to be cooked in an Air Fryer. Similarly, veggies, home-made meals and frozen foods can also be cooked with an Air Fryer. Although they do not have the same cooking instructions with an air fry, they can still be cooked in the Air Fryer.

What kinds of Foods are Not Suitable to be Cooked in an Air Fryer?

Foods that are not suitable to be cooked in the Air Fryer are veggies that require being cooked and steamed for example carrots and beans. You also have to avoid foods that their ingredients will be fried with a batter. Do no cook them in the Air Fryer.

Is it Advisable to Put Oil While Cooking in an Air Fryer?

The answer to this question is yes but you have to combine the oil together with the ingredients. The Air Fryer requires very little amount of oil to completely cook food. It has the capacity to cook food smoothly with only a tablespoon of oil or just a spray of non-stick cooking spray. Research shows that the Air Fryer is the nearest way of cooking that promotes healthy living. If you can cook your food without putting oil, there's no problem about that. You just have to shake the Air Fryer once or twice before the cooking time elapse to avoid sticking.

Are Foods cooked in the Air Fryer Healthy?

Foods that are Air-fried are sumptuous, delicious and healthy. The reality that it makes use of less oil makes it the healthier alternative. Cholesterol and calories contents are in minimal quantities in comparison to other cooking method. Reports have it that there have been some health benefits of eating deep fried foods. Air-Fried foods contain low calories and fats. Some heart diseases like thrombosis and obesity tends to reduce.

Is Air Fryer Similar a conventional oven?

This is somehow complicated. It may be similar but to some extent because there are some things that an Air Fryer does in which an oven cannot do it. Air Fryer can fry and grill, it can deep fry and warms leftover foods. Conventional oven cannot do these things. In terms of size, conventional oven is bigger than Air Fryer. Both conventional oven and Air Fryer have similarities both they are not exactly the same.

Can Air Fryer be Regard to be better than Oven?

The answer to this question could be conceptual base on individual context and usage. Both the oven and Air Fryer have their own specialties. For instance, the air Fryer can cook food faster and save time. It allows for different cooking techniques in order to achieve a sumptuous meal. Conventional oven in the other way round cook's food perfectly and has the capacity to cook large portion of foods. It is not right to say that none is better than the other. They work in their own spectacular way.

Can liquid be used to cook food in the Air Fryer?

Yes, but it all depends on the amount. It must be very small. For instance, you just marinated your fish or chicken, these savory liquids shouldn't be concerned about. It is highly recommended that water should be added regularly when cooking.

My Air Fryer brings out so much smoke. Why?

The smoke coming out while cooking is normal just like you used to cook food in your pan without any oil, it smokes. Same thing is applicable to the Air Fryer. If you cook foods that are high in fat, the fat tends to drain.

Can aluminum foil be used in the power air fryer oven?

The answer is yes! Yes! And yes!!!There are guidelines when using aluminum foil. Do not put the aluminum foil at the bottom of the pan because that is where dirt and all the grease pile up and distort the air circulation. This act affects how your air fryer cooks. Be guided.